Keltic Coloring

KNOTS & NUMBERS

Kathy O'Meara

Perelandra
Design

This book is dedicated
to my Irish/Dutch Family:
Terry, Dennis, Tyche, Crissy, and Michael

Other Books by Kathy O'Meara
Keltic Crosses Coloring
Keltic Alphabet Coloring: Capital Letters
Keltic Alphabet Coloring: Lower Case Letters
Keltic Coloring: Knots & Numbers
Keltic Coloring: Knotted Nature
Stained Glass Window Patterns

International Standard Book Number

ISBN-13: 978-1718817494
ISBN-10: 1718817495

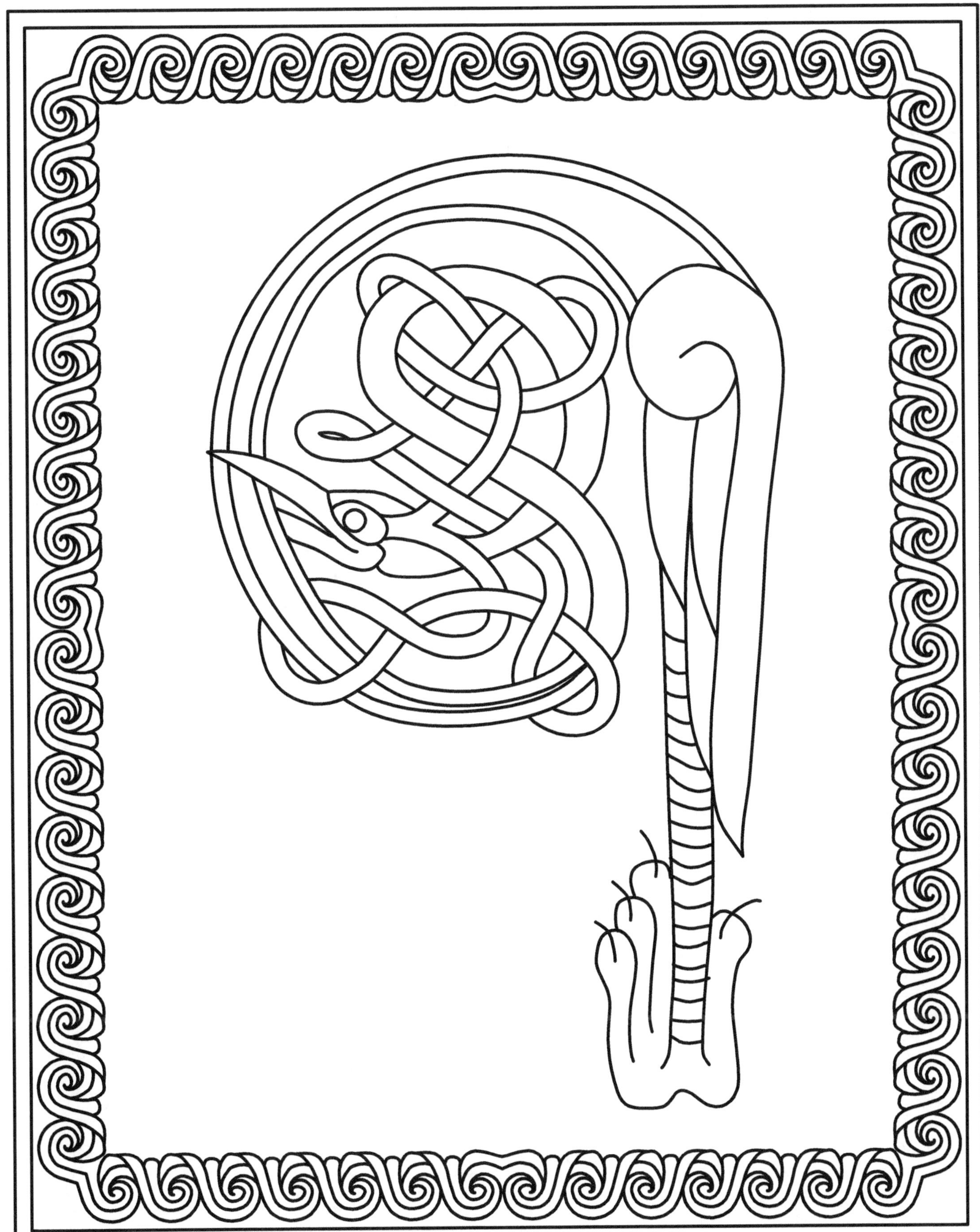